THE CHURCH-ENGLISH DICTIONARY

THE CHURCH-ENGLISH DICTIONARY

The Church-English Dictionary

The Alpha to Omega of Churchspeak

MARTIN WROE, ADRIAN REITH AND SIMON PARKE

Cartoons by Nick Newman

MINSTREL

Eastbourne

First published 1991
Reprinted 1991

Cartoons by Nick Newman

British Library Cataloguing in Publication Data

Church-English dictionary.
1. English wit and humour
I. Wroe, Martin
808.7

ISBN 1-85424-158-3

Printed in Great Britain for
Minstrel, an imprint of Monarch Publications Ltd
1 St Anne's Road, Eastbourne, E Sussex BN21 3UN by
Clays Ltd, St Ives plc.
Typeset by Nuprint Ltd, Harpenden, Herts.

DEDICATION

For Dr George Carey, Archbishop of Canterbury—some light reading for those moments when being Primate of All England gets a little too much.

ACKNOWLEDGEMENTS

Thanks to Nick McIvor, co-author of *The '101' Survivor's Guide to the Church*: the original Church-English Dictionary from that volume is included, if unrecognisably, in the book that follows and Nick had a share in its genesis and genius. Thanks to Simon Jenkins, author of *When Clergymen Ruled the Earth* (Monarch) for letting us reprint a dozen definitions from the late *Ship of Fools* magazine and, to Philip Glassborow for the Harvest sermon. Thanks also to Greenbelters far and wide—the first edition of this book will raise invaluable funds for The Greenhouse project, Greenbelt's all-year-round home.

CONTENTS

SPRECHEN ZE CHURCH?

or

DO YOU SPEAK CHURCH?

The Church-English Dictionary is specially designed to be a straightforward, easy-to-use reference book for the religious, the non-religious or indeed the clergy. Its cleverly devised 'Words-in-alphabetical-order-generally-speaking' format, makes it ideal for work, school, home—or indeed in church, as you sit in your pew with that little but distinctly persistent question knocking on the door of your existence, 'What on earth am I doing here?'

Well, of course, a dictionary can't answer that sort of question. For those seeking existential meaning amid the aimless flux of life, it would be best to go and see someone who is professionally trained in such matters—like a taxi driver.

But in the meantime, there is a related question which this dictionary *can* answer. It's a question which will not be far from your lips if you attend a church or speak with a Christian—and the question is, 'What on earth are you talking about?'

For although 2,000 years of church history have left us with a rich and wonderful heritage of church words, they might be even more rich and even more wonderful if we knew what a few of them meant. This is where *The Church-English Dictionary* comes into its own. 'Do you speak Church?' is a common enough question. With *The Church-English Dictionary* by your bedside, you will proudly be able to reply, 'Yes, I speak Church. Will the Dean be in the Cathedral? My Nave is very well, thank you. But tell me, brother, how are your Sacraments?'

Clearly a reference book of this magnitude and depth doesn't just 'happen'. Research has involved the authors and cartoonist in visiting many hot countries—a laborious task undertaken with enormous endurance and equanimity. They have been particularly keen to pursue the 'Desert Experience'—so crucial to the early formulations of Christian doctrine. The fact that package holiday companies have tended to interpret this more in terms of the 'Beach Experience' has meant deep sun tans and a lot of ice cream for the compilers—but no pleasure. Instead, one can only gasp in amazement at their dogged pursuit of interpretive excellence in far from ideal circumstances. Like deep, sun-kissed sleep for instance.

A further delight in this now classic reference book, is the short English-Church section at the back. It is there especially for the professionally or clinically 'religious'; for those who have been speaking 'Church' for so long now, that they have almost completely forgotten their native tongue. It is, therefore, for those who when asked, 'Can you speak Church?' reply along the lines of 'The Bishop's pew has no hassock,' or 'Let me enjoin righteousness.' When asked, 'Can you speak English?', however, they will look puzzled and flustered and leave hastily muttering, 'Evensong waits for no man,' or, 'I must redeem the time.'

The English-Church section at the back is there to help these people—and they need help—in their first tentative steps back into normal conversation with the English-speaking world.

For the sake of the general reader, footnotes in this edition have been kept to an absolute minimum. There aren't any. As for the word 'etymology', it's a nine-letter word beginning with 'E' (pronounced 'EEEE') which appears in the preface of most dictionaries and therefore the compilers have felt it appropriate to include it in this one.

The
Church-English
Dictionary

apologetics

A little-known sect within the Christian church which apologises a lot.

ascetics

A little-known sect within the Christian church who abound in abasement.

abasement

A room carved out of the ground where you keep the goods for the next jumble sale (*See* A BARGAIN BASEMENT).

apostolic succession

An early form among the apostles of the dance which later became known as 'the conga'. Some are *still* trying to do the 'Apostolic Succession'. Slightly embarrassing.

Augustus Montague Toplady

Perhaps the greatest name found in any hymn book, ancient or modern. The author of that great classic 'Rock of Ages'. Toplady was definitely a top church chap though it is unknown if he shopped at Top Man.

amen

Hear hear. Splendid. Absolutely, old boy! Quite right, too! Yes, yes, yes.

15

alleluia

Term of praise and adoration. Use it to express love for God. Works well sung. (*See also* H for HALLELUJAH.)

angels

God's motorcycle couriers. No request from the Almighty turned down. Not human quite—not divine quite. Can get quite a few on a pinhead. Usually invisible, often turn up just when you need one—but you don't usually realise they were there until they aren't. (NB—some churches don't believe in them, others never think about them, some meet them for breakfast every Tuesday.)

Anglican

Beyond description.

atonement

God declares he is 'at one' with his children. His children respond by being 'at odds' with each other about how exactly God is at one with them. Predictable really... (*See also* ATODDSMENT.)

Amplified Bible

God so loved the world—did you catch that—that he— sorry?—you missed the first word? God, I said GOD—God so loved the world... Oh, never mind! He loves you, all right?

ashes

The body put to bed when the soul goes to play.

aisle

Long narrow bit in-between pews. Often has a bride coming down it. Pronounced—'Aisle have a half.'

apse

A momentary apse of reason through no vault of their own.

army chaplain

A chap with a lot of difficult explaining to do.

absolution

A skin moisturiser used by clergy to soften the hands—if it isn't dry by the end of the service wave your hands in the air up and down and side to side.

archangel

A homeless person who lives under a railway bridge.

Armageddon

The last great battlefield (Rev 16:16). (*See also* SUPERMARKET.) Thought to be derived from the phrase 'Armageddon outta here...'

antiphon

Something to keep the phons away. It is very effective.

awe

Most famously used by the late John Wayne who once played a Roman centurion in the crucifixion scene. In a previous take he had just said, 'Gee, surely this man was the son of God,' and the director suggested, 'Say it with awe, John.' John Wayne then said, 'Aw, surely this man was the son of God.'

awesome

Originally used to designate the might and majesty and magnificence of the Almighty. More recently commandeered by citizens of the United States to describe a powerful human experience. As in, 'That was an awesome cheeseburger.'

awful

Like AWESOME but even more ancient and used to describe the full-of-awe-ness of God. Now used to denote the distinct lack of awe-ness of anything else, as in 'Awful coffee, dear.' But can still be used in the religious sense, eg, 'Another awful sermon from the vicar this morning, dear.'

acolyte

A devoted layman (usually) who carries a candle for a clergyman.

Authorized Version

A seventeenth-century translation of Scripture. It is a work of supreme beauty and clarity, sublime language, marvellous resonance, classic cadences—and quite incomprehensible.

abbey

Place full of habits. Gave birth to the popular expression, 'the Abbey habit'.

abbot

Popular comedian. (*See also* COSTELLO.)

and also with you

A more pious way of saying, 'And the same to you, too.' Most often used when someone turns to you in the Communion service and says something incomprehensible.

all night prayer meeting

Best in middle of June on longest day of year. Usually runs from eleven till midnight. (*See also* HALF NIGHT PRAYER MEETING.)

Ancient and Modern

Ancient.

advent

From the Latin *Ad Verso* which means 'To crowd out God before Christmas with activities of dubious worth.'

arch

Term of intimacy used by Anglican professionals of their earthly boss.

and finally

Term used by preachers about half way through their address.

anthems

Lyrically brief, musically endless.

all-age worship

Worship which *no* age likes very much.

archdeacon

The crook at the head of the Bishop's staff.

ark

Prototype floating zoo.

ASB

Alternative Sermon Book (found in *The '101' Survivor's Guide to the Church*).

antidisestablishmentarianism

A nasty little infection. Take some aspirin and go to bed. Drink plenty of fluids.

antediluvian

The church drains.

anti-charismatic

Someone whose churchmanship is defined by their hostility to the use of certain spiritual gifts. (*See also* CHARISMATIC.)

Ante-Gladys

Relative.

Baptist

A denomination which, instead of using sliced bread or wafers in the Communion service, uses a bap.

baptism

A denomination wherein the bap is elevated above all other breads and cakes, pastries, scones, biscuits and shortbreads. Where sheer baptism is celebrated almost to the exclusion or to the point of denial of the legitimacy of any other breads.

baptism, infant

Service where the very youngest members of the church family, often babies, are introduced to a doctrinal dispute that will mark their entire stay in the church—if they bother to stay.

beard

A useful sign (among the ordained) to the congregation which says, 'I see myself as an Old Testament prophet.'

biblical

Phrase used to imply extra authority to unbiblical views.

Bible-basher

An evangelical who interprets so many things literally in

terms of his Bible, and who is compelled to make endless biblical parallels to every normal daily occurrence, that the Good Book is completely bashed in.

Bible-bender

Process whereby most clerics arrive at their Sunday morning exposition. (So: 'Another Bible-bender this morning, Vicar. I don't know how you do it.')

Bible college

Place where above process can be unintentionally acquired—unless you read the Bible for yourself.

belfry

A useful place to keep your Sunday school superintendents. (*See also* BATS.)

Benedictines

Monks living under the influence of St Benedict, the famous medieval liqueur.

broadcasting, religious

An opportunity for people to put the cat out, make a cup of tea or complete the crossword before the next programme.

bats

Sunday school superintendents over the age of seventy.

beauty

'A wayside sacrament' (Emerson).

Bible

The collected works of God. Believed to explain unusual story—generally known as Life—in which black and white, man and woman, rich and poor all play starring roles in the

strangest script and the longest film and the biggest budget production ever mounted. Unlike other interpretations of Life, Bible version suggests that when they roll the final credits up yonder the 'faith professionals' may end up with key-grip roles (what are they anyway?) while the faith-amateurs may get top billing.

bruised reed

That which God handles with care.

Bruce Reed

Australian fast bowler. English batsmen handle with care.

Bruce Kent

Churchman whose theology led him to give up Holy Orders.

brown study

A place the minister's colourless sermons come from.

blessed

Crucified.

bereavement

Human love letting go into divine love.

bountiful

What we call God when things are going well.

bishop

'It's no accident that the symbol of a bishop is a crook and the sign of an archbishop is a double-cross' (Dom Gregory Dix).

bread

See OFFERING/COLLECTION.

biretta

A hard square hat worn by a hard square clergyman.

burial

What commonly happens to the vicar's sermon over Sunday lunch.

Calvinist

One who believes in designer jeans. (*See also* LEVITES.)

charismatic two-step

Primitive jigging motion lacking obvious co-ordination and rhythm. Common during certain periods of worship referred to as 'time of dancing', as in 'moving into a time of dancing'. (Technical advice: Involves moving from left foot to right foot and back again—with slight hop in between—for several minutes without looking embarrassed.)

canon law

The law that governs the lawless chaos that is the Church of England.

cult

Sunday morning congregations given to wearing overcoats and thick socks and gloves and scarves and long-johns and woolly hats. (*See also* CULT, EXTREMELY.)

conversion

Open heart surgery.

commitment

The burning of bridges.

church growth

Doughnuts after the morning service.

coffin

The final solution to getting out of church.

crematorium

Place where everyone's a smoker but no one gets cancer.

chalice

Goblet, usually silver, used to spread coughs, colds, mouth-ulcers and other orally-dispersed diseases at the end of some services.

chancel

1. Expression of some scepticism: 'Chancel be a fine thing.'
2. Churchy verb to denote indefinite postponement, as in, 'I'm afraid I've had to chancel the WI meeting next Tuesday.'

Church Roof Fund

Money-raising exercise to fill in time until launch of new Restoration Fund Campaign.

crêche

A collision between two cars in Kensington.

Common Prayer, Book of

Collection of unusual prayers.

confession

'To confess your sins to God is not to tell him anything he doesn't already know. Until you confess them, however, they are the abyss between you. When you confess them, they become the bridge' (Buechner).

cassock

Form of ecclesia-wear, usually black or white, with rope around and optional sandals below. Denotes religious convictions of wearer and particularly useful for those who can't get a halo.

church

Generic term for any group trying to be like Christ. Gaggle of geese, tin of spaghetti, church of Christians.

cathedral

Tall building with painted wooden thermometer outside and slogans, for example: '£3m to go!'

chapel

Architectural term to describe video shops and bingo halls throughout South Wales.

church bookstall

A really wonderful place, run by enormously intelligent and discerning individuals whom we have personally admired for a very long time now. Bound to have several copies of *The Church-English Dictionary* prominently—*very* prominently—displayed.

campanology

Study of effeminate vicars.

Candlemas

The next opportunity to light some candles once the wax has finally been scraped off the pews after the carols by candlelight service.

christingle

A moving Christmas service with two classic symbolic moments, 'The Annual Burning of the Children's Hands' and 'The Irredeemable Staining of the Church Carpet with Wax'. It is consequently a service which is enormously popular with adults who aren't church cleaners...

Canterbury

An amazing coincidence—the surname of every single Archbishop for the last ten thousand years.

Carol

One of the few female divines in earlier church history—

given especial prominence in church calendar at Christmas, hence Christmas Carol.

causing to stumble

As used in the sentence, 'We mustn't cause John to stumble.' Means to avoid doing things that seriously disturb someone's faith. In practice, can lead to attempts to please everyone all the time, not rocking the boat, etc.

censer

Someone who regularly uses his cense.

chantry

An endowment so that a poor nobody may croon for the soul of a rich, dead somebody. The origin of soul singing.

chandelier-swinger

Certain kind of revivalist churchgoer prone to wild excitement, often during service of worship—if not before and after. (*See also* TONGUE-WAGGLER, TWO-STEPPER, SPIRITUAL SPACE-KADET.)

christening

A Christian tradition that grew out of a third-century coffee morning in Galatia. Upon discovering that dunking or dipping the digestives made them a good deal nicer, it was decided to do the same with children. Has yet to be proved effective but it's a nice idea—if you're not the child.

celibate

Still looking.

consubstantial/co-eternal

Meaning unknown. First and last used in *Youth Praise 1* (c. 1567).

condemnation

(*See below.*)

condomnation

Used to avoid above.

courage

'Courage is not simply one of the virtues, but the form of every virtue at the testing point, which means at the point of highest reality' (C.S. Lewis).

covering

A church leader whom charismatics must obey. No one knows why. 'He is my covering'—ie, 'I don't have to be responsible for my actions.'

Council of Churches, British

Religious organisation to organise religious unity. Involves different statements of belief of different churches being gradually reduced over period of time until unity is reached. Useful BBC statement of belief: 'We believe in life,' etc.

Council of Churches, World

Like COUNCIL OF CHURCHES, BRITISH, but less explicit.

chasuble

From the Latin *chasius ublo*, meaning 'clothing of the people'. The chasuble is the gorgeous, colourful and highly distinctive over-garment, draped eye-catchingly and stunningly over clergy to indicate just how much they are 'one of us'.

contemplation

Common spiritual gift practised during sermons. Like meditation but spelt differently. Can be mistaken for snoozing.

convention, Christian

The brochure talks of exposure to fresh and stimulating ideas, intense fellowship in the gospel and a time of deep inner renewal. Those attending know it means a warm room to yourself, moderately decent grub and, crucially, three days of freedom from the family.

Coventry

Where you'd like to send half the congregation.

Christmas

The church festival when there continues to be no room at the inn—particularly during Happy Hour.

counsellor

Mmmmmmmmm. Pronounced 'Mmmmmmmm'. From the Hebrew word, 'Hmmmmmm'.

counselling

When two gather for therapeutic pooling of ignorance.

crosier

The staff carried everywhere by the bishop. It is permitted, however, for the staff of frailer bishops, to organise alternative, and probably faster, forms of transport.

concordance

Mixed-up and out-of-order Bible. Only book fatter than the Bible.

church meeting

Regular event where the minister/vicar/pastor tells the congregations what decisions he has made.

curate

Like the deputy manager of your local bank, only really

comes into his own when the manager is on holiday or sick. Sometimes achieves more prominence in the event of a church split—especially if he is leading it.

curate's egg

Curacy is quite a stressful profession, with lots of responsibility but not necessarily any final authority. Can be extremely pressured and, consequently, many curates have lost their hair. Hence curate's egg.

clerical undergarments

Varied, ranging from flared Brutus jeans circa 1974 to chains and locks.

crosses

Formerly symbolised commitment of wearer to the broken God among the thieves. Latterly fashion accoutrement, available in wood, silver, ivory or with a little man on.

convert

Person so embarrassingly excited at being a new Christian they try to make it compulsory for everyone else. Beware of them collaring you in the bus-queue to tell you loudly about their night-life as a prayer warrior.

church advertising

Originally the idea was simple—believers were enjoined to tell someone else about God's love for them in the story of Jesus. If they didn't like it, they might kill you—eg, Stephen, the first martyr.

Later fluorescent church noticeboards were introduced as this usually meant there was less chance of being killed. Unfortunately the slogans put most people to sleep anyway: 'CH..CH—What's Missing? UR.'

Most recently of all, churches have asked advertising agencies to dream up their advertising campaigns for them. Hence: 'Go to Church—it's an act of faith'; 'Party at God's House—wine-music-singsongs-virgins'; 'From Those

Wonderful People Who Brought You Christmas. The
Church of England. His Place. Sunday'; 'Come On Down.
He Does. Why Don't You?' and 'Give Him a Call—Before
You Pay Him a Visit.'

In the US, advertising is more advanced in the church.
An award-winning campaign by the Episcopalian Church
showed St Sebastian tied to a post and shot full of arrows. It
read: 'If you think being a Christian is inconvenient today,
just look back 1,500 years.' Research indicates that the best
advertising is conducted by the best Christians—even
though they may not know it.

Christianise

To make something essentially simple, like 'God loves
people despite their endeavours to be unloved' into
something quite complicated like, 'Are you saved and
washed in the cleansing rivers of blood, my brother?'

Alt meaning: to take out the interesting bits.

Chapel of Ease

Church with ministry to insomniacs.

church mouse

Traditional symbol of absence of earthly wealth as in 'poor
as a church mouse'. Now you can just look at the vicar's
car.

Christianity

Formerly simply called 'The Way'. Now sometimes more
reminiscent of a bus stop.

churchyard

Collection depot for when the dead are raised.

collect

Singular of collection: eg, a ten pence piece.

C.S. Lewis

Mythical figure of spiritual and intellectual perfection

reputed to have all the answers to all the questions.
Supposedly based on Oxford don of the same name.

congregation

Group who gather each week to be reminded why more
people don't go to church.

Alt meaning: the audience; the punters; the paying
public; the pew-fillers; the home-crowd; the fans; the lads.

crusade

Tenth-century mission by the Genghis Khan School of
Evangelism.

compline

What to do during Sunday lunch about how bad the sermon
was.

church lunch

To work properly, the church lunch, which takes place two
or three times a year, depends on a miracle. Members of
the congregation are asked to bring a meat pie or a tin of
pears or a jacket potato—or any item of food of their
choice—to the next week's service, and then everyone is
invited to stay behind afterwards and share food. Even
without the miracle of not ending up with sixty-five
strawberry jellies, another miracle usually occurs—all the
food is invariably eaten. This despite the fact that plates can
include bananas and beans, ice-cream and bean-sprouts,
jacket potatoes and custard, etc.

The church lunch is a symbol of the church community—
you wouldn't think they'd be seen on the same plate
together but, let's face it, they're all going down the same
route in the end.

celebrant

Man at front administering the bread and wine at
Communion who doesn't look as if he has celebrated
anything in a month of Sundays.

chaste

It was St Augustine who first prayed to be chaste—'but not just yet'. Word denotes a state of sexual peacefulness in a person which is the opposite of promiscuity. Might be used in a conversation between two monks under vows of celibacy, as in: 'Chaste any nice girls lately, Fred?'

choir

Keenies, often musical—but not necessarily—usually in robes, found in choir stalls.

chorus

Song with good tune but no theology (*cf* HYMN).

church coffee

Thin, faintly brown substance served after services. Tastes like nothing else. Not recommended.

cross

Some pulpit, some throne.

chapter house

The house where the chaps live.

charismatic (non-religious)

George Best; Prince; Kevin Costner; Greta Scaatchi.

Charismatic (religious)

May require an interpreter if in conversation. Certainly if conversation is with God. Useful to warm up cold churches. Difficult when it all boils over.

collection

Gathering of small change during church service for 'God's work'.

church names

Vary depending on the denomination and the height or depth of churchmanship practised—hence useful to work out whether you want to venture inside or not. 'Zion Tabernacle of Holy Judgement' or 'Ebenezer Chapel of Hellfire and Brimstone' might denote location in South Wales. 'St Mungo Jerry's on the Hilltop' might denote.... While 'The Abundant Wife Fellowship' suggests a polygamous Mormon establishment.

chat

One-to-one, personal sermon.

coffee

See CHAT.

condemnation

Game played by many Christians, but particularly expertly by fundamentalists.

denomination

De nomination of de candidates at de church election.

dog collar

Wall worn around the neck by clergy to separate them from everyone else. Originally 'God Collar'—but wearers couldn't live up to it.

doubt

'Doubts are the ants in the pants of faith. They keep it awake and moving' (Buechner).

deepening work

Phrase often employed to describe an evangelistic project that failed in terms of evangelising, but where the Christians all enjoyed themselves.

divine orders

As in, 'The Lord has told me to marry you.'

divination

A nation preoccupied with the pools.

dedication

A lack of feeling that can come upon a congregation during another particularly boring sermon. Usually starts with a numbing sensation in one's bottom.

deacon

A big orange ball placed upon the top of a black and white stripey pole beside the road. Ignored by everybody. Full name Belisha Deacon.

drama group

A specific kind of group therapy practised in churches that has immense meaning to the participants, but remains hopelessly meaningless (and embarrassing) to the congregation.

dance, sacred

Similar to above. Even worse, though, when dancers raise their arms to reveal large dark sweaty patches that don't seem to help you concentrate on what you should.

dear, old

Any female church member older than you.

dog's breath

That which emanates from just above the dog collar. (*See also* DOG'S LIFE and DOG'S DINNER.)

discipleship

Leaky old vessel that carries the disciples to the other side.

divine

Anything showing God's fingerprints.

dean

As far as cathedrals go he is the Head Honcho. The Boss. The Chief. The Governor. (ie the person who will be cleaning the toilets in heaven.)

dearly beloved

OK, OK, let's have a bit of hush, shall we? I said, *Hush!*
Yes, I'm talking to ye...!

doom

Feeling of many churchgoers in bed on Sunday morning.
Usually followed by more sleep.

death

A fact of life, but not the end of life in the Christian scheme
of things. Generally believed to be final but at least One
exception suggests different rule. Simulated by many church
congregations every Sunday.

deacon

Like a 'gofer' but religious. Basically we...the deacon
is...er...their function, that is—not a dogsbody, no, but
rather, a very real ministry, yes, er...(*see also* CONFUSED).

duty

Job to be undertaken in public view with a look of martyred
resignation.

demon

An angel gone off. Negatively-oriented spiritual power with
friends in low places. Demons may possess individuals who
take them too seriously but have a field day with those who
don't take them seriously at all. Don't take to being laughed
at or anything cross-like being waved in their vicinity.

Eden, Garden of

Where Adam and Eve lost their virginity, naivety and immortality. Alt reading: naked Sunday school in a forest. A particularly useful concept for avoiding the question, 'Well, what was the world supposed to be like?'

epistle

Opposite of a postcard.

elder

Semi-housetrained non-conformist church power-broker. (*See also* SERVANT.) (Ed: 'Why?')

Easter

Commemoration of death of God on a cross symbolised by bunnies and chocolate eggs.

ecumenical

The willingness to be ripped apart that others might be brought together.

ecumanicles

Ecu-manicles are ecclesiastical hand-cuffs kept in reserve during the annual interdenominational service in case the pentecostals get carried away. (Or so they can be carried away.)

evangelical

From Greek meaning 'good news'. Should be a good news kind of person. In theory.

evangelise

To explain the road to salvation in less than one minute without hesitation, deviation or repetition.

eros

Widely assumed to be naughty-but-nice but in fact can merely be extremely nice.

eye for an eye

Old Testament approach to justice still adhered to by many Christians, despite later modification by Christ to more difficult 'turn the other cheek' approach. Also very popular with Muslims.

extempore prayer

Practised by people who don't believe in liturgy—unless it's
their own.

Eggwulf

Bishop of London, 745 AD.

Early Fathers, The

Technically, the 'Late' Early Fathers, as they are all dead.
But still much earlier than us. Though not as early as St
Paul, so perhaps the late Moderately Early Fathers is more
correct. Called 'Fathers' of course, because none of them
were. Purveyors, like most of us, of deep insight and a load
of tosh.

everlasting arms

Said to be 'underneath' and to belong to God. Ideal for
human drop-outs of all kinds. Alt reading: favourite pub in
the new Jerusalem.

Evensong

Formerly a service in the Church of England, now more of
an announcement.

elder

Christian pensioners who run non-conformist
congregations. (*See* WARDEN for Anglican equivalent.)

evangelist

A man (usually) who raises his voice, whom you neither
admire or aspire to be like, who leads you to believe you
should be more like him.

epistle

The weapon you could usefully use to put yourself out of
your misery during an especially boring service.

episcopal

A woozy feeling that comes over a member of the clergy who has just conducted a pre-breakfast Communion service and over-estimated the quantity of wine required. As in, 'Ooooh, I'm feeling all episcopal...'

episcopalian

Chronic practitioner of above.

endowments

Dirty but welcome money in Church of England. (*See also* SSHHH!)

evolution

Sometimes mistakenly spelled evilution—usually by 'biblical creationists'. A faint nagging doubt.

err

Short for Error, formerly Errol—rhyming slang Errol Flynn—Sin. As in 'Father, forgive me for I have Errol Flynned'.

eternity

The nine months from here to maternity.

engagement, speaking

An event in five parts:
1. Hopefully a sherry and a decent meal with the church leader first.
2. The delivery of an old talk dusted down and tarted up with one or two local references.
3. Admiration and thanks from punters.
4. Home in time for mid-week sports special.
5. Quiet, humble anticipation of value of book-token in post.

Eucharist

From the Greek word for 'thanksgiving'. But quite why or how this word has come to describe certain church services is unknown. Perhaps the Greek word for 'earth-shatteringly-boring' didn't slip off the tongue so well.

Egypt

The land out of which the Israelites were rescued. Used metaphorically: 'Brother, are you still in Egypt?' to assess the quality of another's commitment. Beloved in brethren circles. (*See* EGYPT, THE FLESHPOTS OF.)

exhort

It must be 'Stewardship Sunday'.

ex-cathedra

Papal expression. As in: 'I really mean it this time, and I'm not kidding...'

fund-raising

What this book is doing.

fuddy-duddy

See ELDER.

Ford Escort

Official Christian car.

font

Chat-up line from a clergyman. 'Darling, I'm rather font of you...'

funeral

Service where vicar or minister warns you about the eternal damnation awaiting your soul unless you... and tries to tip-toe around the crucial issue of whether the currently coffined subject was the recipient of the necessary amounts of saving grace himself.

funereal

Too many church services.

funeral director

Usually the organist.

Father's Day

Meaningless me-too day inspired by Hallmark Cards.

folk group

A group of folk holding a guitar. No previous musical experience required.

fanatic

Belief overdose.

fantastic

Belief.

fear

Belief underdose.

friendship

What God offers his children.

forgiveness

What you get covered in when you agree.

fashion

Fashion consciousness, in the sense of clothes, is not encouraged in the church because this kind of self-expression draws attention to oneself—which naturally is undesirable—and the contours of the body can cause trouble. The ideal apparel in church is a shapeless sack.

Fulk Basset

Bishop of London, 1244 AD.

faith

All good Christians need this—the oxygen of the spiritual life—you gasp and give up without it. Contrary to popular teachings, the Christian idea is not about faith in a bunch of 'doctrines' dreamt up by early church daddies, but in the closeness of Jesus, in the goodness of people despite our badnesses, in the conviction that despite all the evidence to the contrary, at some point God will sit everyone down and say, 'Look, I can explain everything.' (*See* FRIENDSHIP.)

faith

The outstretched hand.

fat

The outstretched stomach.

Father of the Bride

Proud-looking man in the outsized top and tails, with a bride on his arm.

fete (sic)

What you believe in if you can't be bothered to pray.

fullness of time

Never.

fellowship

Group of people who enjoy talking about each other. Oddly enough used by Paul the Apostle only in context of 'suffering'; *cf*: 'fellowship of sufferings'.

fundamentalist

Somebody who understands everything.

fun

What fundamentalists fundamentally don't have.

flower rota

A sheet of paper so that the flowers know when they're on duty.

flannelgraph

A modern, hi-tech method (in 1888) of communicating the gospel in Sunday school using coloured card figures with tea towels on their heads who constantly fall off a board covered with felt. The flannel is provided by the teacher. The children are generally captivated... by the way the figures don't stick.

fool

Anyone who follows Jesus Christ.

bonkers

Anyone who decides against. (Publisher: 'Er, F for Bonkers, boys?')

friar

I suppose a Tuck is out of the question?

gateway to glory

Dying.

Greek

As welcome as Jew.

Greek, all to me

Quite a lot of sermons.

groin

Architectural word describing the edge formed by
intersecting vaults, or the fillet used to cover this edge. So,
extra careful with the duster at the next church spring clean.

GNB

Bible fully illustrated with curly stick people.

gargoyle

1. Bizarre and often hideous old weatherbeaten face carved
out of stone high up in cathedrals. (*See also* BISHOP.)
2. *See also*, or rather, hear also—sound emanating from
choir vestry before the sung Eucharist.

guided tour

Common in cathedrals and large historic church buildings.
Function: to fill gaps in between services and in church roof.

glossolalia

The gift of saying incomprehensible and strange words. Incomprehensible and strange words like, er, 'glossolalia' for instance.

glory, God's

Something Christians are asked to reflect. Best reflections obtained by believers setting themselves at the right angle.

Godspell

Good musical, long running but expensive.

gospel

Good news, even longer running—and free.

gifts of the Spirit

Originally conceived to aid the Christian's task of making the world better. Latterly used more commonly to have church splits over. (*See* ANTI-CHARISMATIC.)

Gideons

An association of Christian businessmen with terrible memories. They've left their Bibles in hotel rooms all over the place.

gaiters

Nasty things that crawl out of swamps and bite you.

grief

Love left over at the end.

guitar

Unique stringed instrument, modified for use with three chords only, found in many churches. Believed by many to be created by God for youth services.

God

Three letter word. Without which there would be no book in your hand, no hand on your arm, no arm on your body, no body...er...no...er...well...etc. Christian view is that God made everything up to start with and continues to make up everything as he goes along. In other words, if he decided he'd had enough we wouldn't know it because we'd have been unmade up before we realised it.

The fact that our world is still here is testimony to God's penchant for what the Book calls 'longsuffering'. After all, just because God is a three letter word does not mean that he is not also a four letter word—LOVE. Confusing, eh? But that's God all over for you. Miraculous.

Godparent

Usually male, Italian, bearing sub-machine gun in violin case. May attempt to wipe you out.

genuflection

Momentary cramp in front of the altar. Getting down on one knee and nodding at the holy table usually helps relieve pain.

Gospel

Good news.

Michael Buerk

Nine O'Clock news.

guilt

A trusted retainer we keep on, because he's easier to handle than God's love.

Gabriel

An archangel. Also the sort of person most churches are seeking to appoint as their new minister or priest.

Godparents

Know anyone whom you can imagine still being on speaking terms with in, say, ten years' time? Choose them.

habit

Divers uses: heroin addiction to cloister-garb.

hat

A strange form of gag. It is said that when one is stuck on a woman's head in some churches, it stops her from speaking.

healing

See GP—GREAT PHYSICIAN.

Healing Broadway

Last stop on the Central Line.

however

The watershed in any evangelist's prayer letter. Before this point, the latest mission is described in glowing terms. After it comes 'the urgent need for our practical provision'.

house church

1. People who throw off religiosity by meeting and worshipping in a home setting to develop their own particular religiosity.
2. Church with no pulpit, no pews and no neighbours.

house-church music

Reason the neighbours left.

house music

Popular form of music as eighties turned into nineties.
Likely to enter church life in a century or two.

holy orders

What Roman Catholics get if the Pope speaks ex-cathedra.
(*See* EX-CATHEDRA.)

holy marching orders

What they get if they ignore him.

healing

The human desire, the divine possibility, the ultimate
reality.

holy smoke

The sight of your huge church building burning down
through an act of vandalism and the thought of the warm,
specially designed community centre you can create with
the insurance payment.

holy smoke, Batman

The Boy Wonder on seeing the above.

holy inappropriate

What the actress said to the bishop.

Heathoberht

Bishop of London, 794.

honk

That which car stickers in the USA encourage us to do if we
love Jesus.

honky

Presumably, someone who follows the advice of the above-mentioned car stickers.

hatch, match, dispatch

Friendly ecclesiastical terms indicating the reasons that most people have for trespassing on church property.

hot air

Cheap internal heating system for churches but only works if you're sitting near the pulpit.

hot prot

See PROT, HOT.

honour

What you give God if you live like Jesus.

half night of prayer

Nine till midnight including songs (one hour), sharing (one hour) and coffee (forty-five minutes).

house of the Lord

An ordinary building in which people behave extraordinarily.

heart attack

What happens just before you get up to read the lesson.

heart failure

What happens after you sit down when you realise you've just read the wrong lesson.

hallelujah

Has different meanings in different contexts—from 'praise God', to 'err', to a swear word.

hope

A stirring deep within as the preacher says, '...and finally.'

horoscope

An optical instrument shaped rather like a kaleidoscope with a view of naughty things.

heaven

The complete presence of God and the complete absence of the Scoutmaster.

hell

Vice-versa.

hell

A good word for a bad place.

heaven

A bad word for a good place.

hassock

See NARTHEX.

Harvest Festival

One of the great seasons in the church's calendar when
churchgoers bring food they don't want to be dispersed to
non-churchgoers who don't want it either. Sermons are
preached, of course. Here is an example of a sermon that
you might like to pass on to a friendly cleric for his Harvest
delivery:
'Feast of the Holy Marrow.'
My dear people, it is time once more for us to celebrate
Harvest Festival—or as the dear bishop roguishly insists on
calling it, the Feast of the Holy Marrow. You will no doubt
have already seen the display at the back of the church,
which this year includes—rather appropriately, I thought,
considering the setting—a loaf of Sunblest.

There are also two courgettes from Mr Lumsdale, or
rather from his allotment, although they are also in a very
real sense from Mr Lumsdale, and ultimately of course,
from God. And that is surely one of the messages of harvest
time—that we have God to thank and Mr Lumsdale for his
provision, or rather provisions.

Which brings me to my next point—baked beans.
Forming part of the display, you will see a tin of baked
beans which I will be distributing among the poor old folk
of the parish. Poor old folk indeed, if that's all they're
getting this year. And so I have taken my text this year, not
from the Bible, but from the bean tin itself.

I hope you all read your Bibles regularly—and also your
bean tins, too, which also keep you regular in a very real
sense. Here on the tin I read the words 'permitted

flavouring', and it is encouraging, I think, to remember that in this life (of which variety is the spice) flavouring is indeed permitted. So often the church seems to be saying, 'Thou shalt not do this, that or the other—especially the other.' But here we are saying at this rejoiceful time of year that flavouring is permitted.

Which brings me to my next point—modified starch. Let us all try to bear in mind—particularly we clergy—that if we have indeed allowed any starch into our lives, and it's something we all do, I know I do—let us indeed modify it.

Finally let us take heart from these few words, 'Best Before End...' This little phrase can tell us so much, and may I leave you with that thought tonight.

hallelujah, brother/sister

Term of pleasure denoting Almighty as benefactor in this instance.

Hymns for Today's Church

Yesterday's, actually.

Hebrew

The language the angels speak, unlike Welsh—the language God speaks. The gift of tongues may be a theological debating point on earth but it's compulsory in heaven. How else did you think you were going to have that argument with Paul about women wearing hats? (*See also* SIXTEENTH-CENTURY ENGLISH.)

High Church

The wing of the church led by slightly bitter, failed actors who still want to appear in a 'show'. Lots of dressing up and props, 'G&Ts' and 'Marvellous performance, darling', plus an adoring if dwindling audience.

holy

In communion with God.

humble

In a right relationship with your neighbour.

human

Someone who finds humble and holy rather difficult.

heresy

Disagreeing with His Holiness the Pope (Roman Catholics), John Calvin (the Free Presbyterians), the Ayatollah Khomeini (lots of Muslims) or John Stott (evangelicals).

hermeneutics

Like Herman and the Hermits but not a sixties pop group.

heterosexual

1. What you need to be to keep out of trouble in most mainline denominations.
2. Someone pretending they're all right sexually.

hope

The lived belief that with God no situation is the end of the story.

humans

At once 'the glory and the scum of the universe' (Blaise Pascal).

High Church

1. St Paul's Cathedral.
2. Those with a high view of the sacraments. Certainly over six feet, anyway.

Hi!

Expression of chumminess common to evangelical Anglican vicars as they meet you in the street. (Pronounced: 'Hiiiiiyyyyyyyyyyyyy!')

hymn

Song with good theology but no tune (*cf*, CHORUS).

her indoors

Where many Christian hims believe that Christian hers should be kept.

Holy Spirit

God's kiss.

invitation

I want you to get up out of your seats...Billy Graham's way of ending a meeting. (Don't worry—your coaches will wait.)

intercession

Standing in other people's shoes in God's presence.

itinerant

Someone who has problems with long-term relationships as in 'itinerant evangelist' or an 'itinerant teaching ministry'.

icon

Pictures of saints generally doing slightly odd things with their fingers. But surrounded by gold to remind us that flesh was made for glory. So hang in there!

incense

God's Chanel No 5. Human special effects to give the impression of God's presence. Verb: to make angry by choking someone to death. People who do this regularly are considered incredibly incensitive.

inscrutable

God knows. (*See* UNSCREWING THE INSCRUTABLE.)

incumbent

Incorrect name for a parish priest. (*See* RECUMBENT.) To lie down. To take one's ease. Repose.

inquiry

What parishioners make concerning baptisms.

inquisition

What inquiry turns into when clergyman discovers little Barry isn't a member of the Sunday school. As in, 'Thankfully, Mrs Smith, the days of the Inquisition are over, but really, there are still questions I must ask and which you must answer'...etc, etc.

induction

1. A service wherein an incumbent-to-be is compelled (or INDUCED) to take a living.
2. The special service marking the arrival of a new clergyman in the parish. He is induced by the bishop who acts as 'midwife' and also provides the gas.

implausible

That which is intrinsically unbelievable or unlikely. Like a bald hair tonic salesman. Like a church leader who can laugh at himself/herself.

immersion, total

How to become a baptist, total. The Total Baptists are the movement from which came the Total and Utter Baptists. They of course believe in Total and Utter Immersion. Not many survive this, which means that Total and Utter Baptists are not a large group.

I

Common in extemporaneous prayers as in: 'I really just want to say, Lord...'

infallible

Incapable of error.

Ian Paisley

See INFALLIBLE.

Isn't it lovely?

Term used in spring/summer as churchgoers enter/leave the service, to fill in silences. Thought to refer to weather.

introit hymn

Hymn sung in Anglican churches at the start of the service, as the priest enters. By the last verse, even some of the congregation are arriving.

incarnation

Difficult theological word to describe God's move from the lofty heights of the Godhead, heaven, Lord of the universe and all that... to the belly of a Jewish girl and life as a creature like the rest of us. Concept of the Holy Spirit to be precise.

joy

Something that is very deep in the Christian experience. Very deep indeed. So deep, in fact, that it is generally invisible.

Jerusalem

Favourite wedding hymn that sounds fantastic and says nothing that anyone understands.

judgement

You are invited by the Queen to a great feast at Buckingham Palace. On your arrival, you are courteously ushered into the great banqueting hall. You are stunned by the colour of the occasion and the care that has been put into it. You also rather regret that you are standing there in an old T-shirt and wearing paint covered trousers, having come straight from redecorating your living room. It's not that anyone *says* anything, but there is a loud voice inside you, screaming, 'Aaaargh, I wish I was somewhere else...'

James, King Version

Put his name to a best-seller.

jeans, stonewashed

Anticipated form of clergy trouser-wear in year 2000.

jeans, flared

Current form of clergy trouser-wear.

jeans, engineering

When scientists mess with your jeans to try and cure diseases.

junior church

Special section of ecclesiastical community targeted at those in church below sixteen and aimed at ensuring they're not there afterwards.

journey to church

The longest journey.

journey to God

The shortest.

jumble sale

Financial engine-room of the modern church. Without it the church would be plunged into the red. Also useful when books are balanced: while most church accounts are teetering on bankruptcy, once the socks, knickers and left shoes are marked down as assets, the accounts are immediately in the black again.

just

(*See* i for i.)

Jesus

God's self-portrait.

joyful noise

The sound of musicians who can't play.
Alt meaning: the sound of the church organ beginning the last verse of the last hymn on Sunday morning.

justice

What love wants.

joke, good

A tiny revolution, derailing pomposity, exposing prejudice.

joke, bad

An exercise in conformity, massaging pomposity and confirming prejudice.

joke, Christian

(*See* JOKE, GOOD and JOKE, BAD.)

kneeler

Someone who prays a lot.
Alt meaning: small piece of furniture found in churches to avoid knee-capping of fervent pray-ers.

knave

He who should be in the NAVE.

kiss of peace

What married couples do at the end of the sulk that has come after the row.

koinonia

Christian coffee-shop in Warrington.

kingdom of God

Where the poor are given riches, the mighty humbled, the hungry fed, the vain disillusioned, the naked clothed, the blind given sight and there's dancing all night long to 60s soul music. Christians live on its edge, in love with the idea but scared of the consequences. The kingdom is here but not all here—unlike Christians who are often here but not all there. You can hear the kingdom on a good day. It's the sound of angels playing in a gospel combo, of saints marching in. The sight of all the colours bleeding into one.

Keswick

Evangelicaldom's Lourdes.

kink

Not sure how this word crept in. It has nothing at all to do with the church.

King, Burger

Cheap fellowship meal.

kong

Congregational.

katalambanomai

A moderately long and possibly quite important Greek word which a decent dictionary would probably attempt to define.

karaoke

Experimental Japanese services.

Kama Sutra

Not allowed.

Levite

One who believes in designer jeans. (*See also* CALVINIST.)

liturgical dance

1. Name given to embarrassing displays of sweaty armpits in church especially by people who can't dance.
2. Often done by Christian women in shapeless flowery skirts (*see* LAURA ASHLEY). The origins of this strange practice are obscure but it could date back to 1963 when the Knit-A-Kneeler parish project was completed at St Novelty's, thus leaving women with shapeless flowery skirts rather short of activities.
(Pronounced: 'What are those strange people doing up at the front, Dad? Have they got something in their shoes?')

laid aside

Used to describe a person who is unwell. It should be noted that the correct form of this phrase is 'laid aside' and not the unfortunate variation, 'lying on one side in a bed of sickness'.

laid on my heart

Roughly translated, this phrase means that God has caused an individual to be concerned about a particular need or situation. Avoid using, 'I've had leprosy laid on my heart,' etc.

liturgy

An order of words designed for the congregation to fall back on when they can't concentrate in church. In regular use.

lay

A church helper. Who does the lay person help? The *recumbent*, of course. (*See* INCUMBENT.)

lay reader

An ordinary person in the Anglican church who is specially licensed by the bishop to help out the Recumbent with church duties...er...except those duties which require extra special knowledge or qualifications...like praying over bread and wine.

lie

'Lovely sermon, Vicar.'

lectern

The place from where the reading isn't heard, week by week.

Laura Ashley dresses

Useful indication as to who the minister's wife is. (*See* LAURA ASHLEY—official couturier to the church-going classes.)

lead (service)

To conduct a service. Host. Presenter. Master of Ceremonies. Life and Soul. Conductor. Number One Man (usually). Often goes down like a (*see below*) balloon.

lead (church roof)

(*See* RELIGIOUS ORDER.)

Lord

Used regularly to punctuate extemporaneous prayers—in case God forgets that he is being addressed. As in, 'We do just ask, Lord, that Lord, you will, Lord, bless, Lord, our Sunday school outing, Lord.'

last times

Periodic occasions in history when the world ended—until it didn't. After which its proponents revise their theology and renew their pension scheme.

Lady Chapel

Wife of Lord Chapel and mother of little Sunny Chapel. Specially ordained for worship, unlike most ladies in chapel.

love

Rare substance. Believed to be what God is made out of. And what he made people out of.

love making

What people make people out of.

light

What sermons generally obscure.

Lent

Season in church calendar when lots of things can be given up in order to rededicate one's life to the Lord—like money for example. Hence the expression, 'Lent us a fiver.'

lost, the

People outside Sainsbury's on Saturday mornings being shouted at by men in sandwich boards and funny haircuts.

litany

Shopping list.

Lord's, the house

The house nobody else wants because God must be the only one who can afford to heat it.

Lords, not the house

Home of cricket.

lust

'The craving for salt of a man who is dying of thirst' (Buechner).

Low Church

No pictures, no candles, no colour. The same effect can also be achieved by walking around with a large bucket over your head.

Morris Thousand

Christian car until advent of Ford Escort. (*See* THOUSAND, ONE HUNDRED AND FORTY-FOUR.)

multi-purpose plant

A tulip with conference facilities.

monk

Fat, bald, terrible clothes, no money—and generally laughed at. But when you're discovering the love of God through a life of prayer, such matters are fairly secondary.

Moderator

A church leader who wears a Parka and rides a Lambretta.

missal

Object for hurling at dull preachers.

monastery

Monk factory for mass-production of good habits.

mountain-top

A feeling of euphoria, especially after participating in a large-scale Christian event. To be 'on the mountain-top' is the opposite of being 'in the valley'.

miracle

When a human obeys God.

modern translation

Translation of the Bible that goes out of date every year.

ministry

Anything a Christian does.

ministry, my

Whatever I want to do.

ministry, your

Whatever I want you to do.

minister

Confusing word for a non-conformist vicar.

minister, to

Serve, care for. Occasionally seen in above.

miniskirt

Any skirt above the ankle. Discouraged.

modernist

Lostinthemist.

macho

(*See* MUSCULAR CHRISTIANITY.)

mission

Impossible.

meditation

The bits in a service when nothing happens and people stare

at the floor. Often used to pad services out to a decent length. No preparation required.

man

Sometimes seen in church, but not nearly as common as wo-man.

manse

Hovel where minister now lives.

mansion in the sky

House minister is moving to. (*Cf* MANSE IN THE SKY and LUCY IN THE SKY WITH DIAMONDS.)

maracas

A favourite musical instrument of church music groups. Delightfully simple in design. Impossible to make sound attractive.

maturity

Integration.

mount

Any biblical hill.

matins

On the floor to wipe your feetins.

matrimony, holy

State preceding Bliss, Wedded. 'It has been said that a bride's attitude towards her betrothed can be summed up in three words: Aisle, Altar, Hymn' (Frank Muir).

marriage

Invented by God to create an environment strong enough to contain laughter, despair, sex, routine, anniversaries, children, honesty, crisis, dishonesty, and in-laws. (Pronounced: 'Now that's what I call a holy institution.')

monogamy

'Christians are only allowed one wife and this is known as monotony' (Schoolboy).

mitre

An enormous gold crown-like creation, worn by the bishop to indicate deep humility.

maturity

What you don't need to write this book.

mount up with wings...

Climb onto a stage with Paul McCartney—theological
implications unclear. Alt reading: to receive an unexpected
cheque in the post.

man of God

Heavenly ranking bestowed while on earth. Just after MAN
OF PRAYER.

Man-God

Jesus.

Methodist

Unique approach to church-going pioneered by Robert de
Niro-Wesley, known commonly as 'Methodist Acting'.

my yolk is easy

Yes, but you don't tell 'em very well and you always mess
up the punchline...

moving into

Directional expression as in: 'Moving into a time of prayer/
singing/having coffee/sleep...' etc.

mind

Something many churchgoers have mistakenly believed they
must hang up in the lobby on their way in to services. In
fact Christianity is about wholeness which includes the
development of everything up in your skull. A Christian
mind ought not to sound a contradiction in terms.

male

A slightly smaller version of what God is—according to
most men in church.

Mothering Sunday

The day in memory of St Interflora who is the patron saint of capitalistic wheezes.

muscular Christianity

A movement within the church which seeks to add testosterone to the Thirty-Nine Articles. (*See also* SLIM FOR HIM.)

Nunc dimittis

Now, dimwits.

nervous breakdown

Common experience of most clergymen after about four or five months in the job. Thought to be brought on by combination of inflated sense of own abilities and discovery that parishioners are all fully-paid-up members of Monster Raving Loony Party.

non-conformist

Conformist.

novice

A baby monk, a little monkey.

nuncio

Nunsense.

Nuptual Mass

What you have before you have the Nuptual Mess.

nunderwear

What they wear under their habits.

noticeboard

Wooden contraption bearing angry fluorescent poster, found outside many church buildings. Can often be seen displaying the coded message: 'Jn 3:16' which means 'there is a fire-hydrant near here somewhere'. Or 'CH..CH— WHAT'S MISSING? UR' Good eh?

noticebored

Response of most passers-by.

narthex

Abusive term indicating crass stupidity. As in, 'You steaming great narthex! I said kneel on my hassock, not my cassock!'

nave

The main body of the church. Named after the main body of the occupants. (*See* KNAVE.)

NIV

Abbreviated term for the Bible used by many fundamentalist Christians, the Nearly Infallible Version.

Nicene Creed

The only fourth-century invention we're still using.

no

Word believed by many non-Christians to define Christianity. And by many Christians.

numinous

A sense of God's presence. Good Nu's.

numerous

A sense of everybody else's presence. Not always good Nu's.

organ

Large Victorian pipe-instrument with fat lady on it at front of house.

Open Brethren

Open Sesame, but...er...not quite, so Open Sesa*her*.

open our hearts

Stop talking will you?!

old man

1. Your father.
2. A phrase used to describe the pre-Christian you.

offering

That's you in theory.

open heart surgery

(*See* CONVERSION.)

open wallet surgery

That's you in practice.

ordination

Two things happen at ordination.
1. Hands are laid on the candidate's head.
2. His backbone is removed.

open air evangelism

Involves embarrassing passers-by in the street with incomprehensible jargon found mainly in this book. Lurid banners may be used. Terrible music may also be used. In fact anything and everything may be used—including you.

original sin

It's extremely hard these days to commit sins with any degree of originality. But it doesn't stop us trying.

Obadiah

Not so much a minor prophet in the Old Testament, as a really minimal one. Bless him.

offertory

Anglican contribution to the Conservative Party.

Omphalosceptic

Navel gazer. Usually used by, and of, theologians.

office

Most people go *to* it. Clergy *say* it.

oratorio

An American biscuit.

order

What you feel like shouting in some charismatic churches.

orders, holy

Another posh name for an ordinary minister.

orders, last

What you hope the service will finish before.

papal bull

He said it.

parking space

This is the most prayed-for concept in Christian theology. Believed to be a kind of Nirvana-like state wherein are focused all kinds of accumulated hopes and fears. Confusion with Eastern thinking often creeps in here because even though Christian theology allows no sense of deserving special treatment—when it comes to the parking space it is sometimes felt that one is 'owed' one, considering that you were just pipped at the post for the last two spaces and you really are in a terrific hurry to get on with the Lord's work.

Passover

The ancient but now less common tradition of 'passing over' priests who were not masons in the promotion stakes.

peace

Unusual substance, believed to be what God is made of. (*See also* LOVE.)

peace of Christ

Available on request from all good church stockists.

piece of Christ

What Christians should be like.

paunch

'Filled, pressed down and running over' (Luke 6:38).
Biblical reference to clergy trousers. Maybe that's why they
invented cassocks.

pooch

The one on whom you blame that unpleasant smell during
the home Bible study.

pouch

A cunning device sometimes passed round instead of a
collection plate that makes it much harder to get money out
than to put it in. Congregation please have the correct
money ready.

peculiar

A place exempt from the jurisdiction of the bishop of the
diocese in which it is situated, eg St George's Chapel,
Windsor. If, however, it is only partially exempt, it is only a
bit peculiar. (*See also* ODD, A TRIFLE.)

photographs, wedding

Popular if lengthy tradition which often happens after a
short service which no one is really interested in. Useful tip:
the longer the photographs take, the smaller the spread
afterwards is likely to be.

pneumatology

The study and classification and collection of road drills.

prophet

Someone who gives God ten out of ten and humans about
two-and-a-half.

priest

Someone who gives God ten out of ten and humans the benefit of the doubt.

prophecy, to make a

To charge ten when it costs you nothing. (*See* THATCHERISM.)

preaching with a view

1. The preacher views the congregation, the deacons, the boiler, the sisterhood and the cracked cups with an eye to becoming the pastor of the church.
2. The congregation views the preacher, his sermon and his devotion to *The Baptist Hymn Book* with an eye to voting him in.

profit

Er, not relevant in a book about the church. (*See* JUMBLE SALES for ecclesiastical fiscal policy.)

Pope, the

His Holiness to a billion Roman Catholics. 'The Beast' to Ian Paisley.

promoted to glory

Dead. Passed away. No more. Gone to meet his Maker. Cheesed. Popped his clogs. Six feet under and pushing up daisies.

presence, God's

Like a winter coat. It won't affect the chill weather, but it will affect how you view it.

parousia

If you are standing in a bookshop parousia-ing this book— jolly well buy it.

pew

Extremely hard substance which has formed over millions of years into incredibly uncomfortable shapes. It was thus ideal for church seating, to which it gave its name.

pulpit

Ecclesiastical furnishings designed to enable user to look down on everyone else.

parable

Earthly story, heavenly meaning—and the devil to interpret sometimes.

Plymouth Brethren

Several men who lived on the south coast and founded this well-known religious sect. They believed that when you die your soul goes to Plymouth—as long as your wife wore a hat and didn't talk in church.

prayer circle

Like sewing circle but no sewing machines.

preacher's hump

What the minister gets after persistent criticism of his sermons. (*See also* TENNIS ELBOW, WRITER'S BLOCK, etc.)

prayer chain

Religious variant on chain letter. Lots of people send messages to God in hope of winning extraordinary prize.

prayer mat

A sort of flying carpet.

Allied Carpets

Where the prayer mats are stored.

pilgrimage

That long forgotten age when there were pilgrims.

prot, hot

What happens to missionaries among cannibalistic tribes.

penance

Sorry plus something.

pastor

Abbreviation for use when dining. As in 'Pastor sauce, pastor butter, pastor spuds...'

preaching scarf

Worn by key members of congregation to indicate support for preacher. Can be waved in air during communal singing as in 'Come on, you Rev...'

passage, rite of

Corridor that leads us to fresh views.

PCC

Group of geriatric Anglicans who agree to the incumbent's every whim.

peace

The bit of the Communion service when you try to appear interested in the person next to you. Or when you suddenly develop a momentary paralysis.

parish

A clergyman's patch or manor.

parish magazine

The magazine that doesn't reach the clergyman's patch or manor.

prayer

A list of ultimatums given to God when all other avenues have been exhausted.

parade service

Theological nightmare. Community development dream.

photographer

Failed Butlin's Redcoat in search of a captive audience. (*See* WEDDINGS.)

priests

(*See* M for MALE.)

platonic, purely

Denotes relationship between a couple in which there is no time for sex because they're too busy discussing philosophy.

Presbyter

'New Presbyter is but Old Priest writ large' (Milton).

Presbyterian

Ask Milton about this one.

Frisbeeterians

Small but growing religious sect which believes that when we die our souls get stuck on the roof and we can't get them down again.

plastic cups

Created by God to ensure no one stays after the service. (*See* CHURCH COFFEE.)

provost

A small tool for cutting the hairs that grow out of the nose and ears.

Pentecostal

When God sets his friends on fire.

predestination

Theological term that hit the big time in the fifteenth and sixteenth century. Little used as an idea these days. Probably doomed from the start.

poor, the

Blessed, the

psalm enchanted evening

When to propose a marriage made in heaven.

quinquennial

Sea sickness tablet, mostly used for walking on water.

quenching

What not to do with the Holy Spirit.

Queen

Non-sexist King substitute as in 'We three queens of orient are'.

quiet time

Ancient Christian ritual which involves making a cup of coffee, taking out a Bible, trying to find a comfy chair, wondering who to pray for, saying 'Amen' and going to the launderette.

quite awful

Like QUIET TIME but more common.

questions

What you get if you become a Christian.

recumbent

(*See* INCUMBENT.)

cucumber

(*See* SANDWICHES.)

renewal

Don't overlook this if you're hoping to claim your eternal life assurance.

revival

What you need at the end of a particularly boring revival meeting.

Richard of Beaumes II

Bishop of London, 1152.

RSV

Really Stuffy Version...but not quite so archaic as the KJV.

RSVP

Special edition commissioned by The Polite Society.

right hand of fellowship

1. An announcement made before more liberated church services: 'Will patrons please note that the right hand of the fellowship has been designated a no-smoking area.'
2. What the deacons give you when you enter into membership of a Baptist church.

repentance

(*See* YOU TURN.)

reformation

A rearrangement of people into an arrangement that then needs rearrangement.

religious

Conscientiousness. The pastor religiously turns up at the church but the local people religiously stay at home and religiously wash their cars.

restoration scheme

Bid for self-worth by slightly depressed church leader.

relic

The old person, usually called Miss Thrush, who is the reason why nothing ever changes at St Botolph's. As in: 'We could never do that—think of Miss Thrush.'

retreat

The advance into silence.

reserved sacrament

'I'm sorry, madam, but this sacrament is reserved. Perhaps there's another one I could interest you in?'

revival day

In a tent. Strange, noisy ritual that involves a visiting soloist, guest preacher, and the endless 'invitation'. The participants generally start in the back row, sitting, and end up kneeling or lying in front of the front row, weeping.

revival week

Necessary when above revival weak.

revivalist preacher

Man in a tent trying to force the hand of God.

Revelation

Complicated bit at the back.

rite

The order of service that helps you deal with your wrongs. (*See* WRONGS.)

ritual

Common ecclesiastical procedures, such as making sure the

church is freezing, has hard seating and no toilets, that the clergy speak in incomprehensible voices, deliver very boring sermons and invite you to stay for horrible coffee afterwards.

ritualistic sacrifice

What the congregation feels like when subject to the above.

Roman Catholic

A multicoloured firework that explodes at regular intervals.

Roman Candle

How the Pope reads after lights out.

racism

The organisation of prejudice.

Redemption Hymnal

A popular hymnal in non-conformist churches that needs to be redeemed.

rhyme

Used at the end of lines in many hymns, most popularly with variant orderings of the words, Refiner's Fire, Desire and Higher, etc.

really

Term of emphasis used by people who believe that God is in a hurry. Accordingly the pray-er cannot stop for breath or even to think of an interesting adjective as he/she makes representations before the throne of grace. Instead they insert the word 'really' every couple of words: 'We really love you...'; 'I really just ask that you will...'; 'Just really bless our time tonight...'

rally

> 1. As previous entry except used in posher churches. 'Oh, Lord, we rally bless your name...'
> 2. Events, often open air, organised by Christians to spread the good news to people who have yet to take note of it— or even any notice of it. Usually with loud speaker— quietly spoken evangelists can use a microphone—and often in a big park. Common themes: Sin, Sin and Sin. Lots of singing. If the rally is evangelistic then it often climaxes in altar call. (*See* A for ALTAR CALL.) If not evangelistic there is often no climax at all.

royally

> As in, 'loife of'.

resurrection

> Post-death experience pioneered by Jesus Christ, now widely available from all good churches.

ripe unto harvest

> Term of description for fertility—or otherwise—of soul of pagan contact. As in, 'Should get him saved soon...'; 'She's on the brink...'

right on!

> The status of being OK! Cool! In touch! Stylish! Seriously relevant! Yes sireee! Sweet as a nut!

Right Hon

> The status of some Anglican bishops. Nothing like the above.

redemption

> God's idea.

religion

> Man's idea.

Reformed

Often Scottish or German. Strict. Talk about John Calvin a lot.

religious order

'Here you—come down off that church roof now!'

reconciliation

'I'm in power and you better get reconciled to it!' (Alinsky).

raptured

To be snatched bodily up to heaven.

ruptured

What happens if you get raptured in an awkward position.

rota

List of those due for rapture.

sacrifice

1. Agreeing to be put on a rota.
2. 'To sacrifice something is to make it holy by giving it away for love' (Buechner).

second blessing

The blessing in between the first blessing and the third blessing and two before the fourth. Pronounced: 'Storm in a tea-cup.'

symbol

Like the Tardis, symbols tend to be bigger inside than they look from the outside. Great symbols, like the cross, will take a life-time to explore.

secretary, church

Common in Free Churches. Elderly gent with shaky hand and wobbly notes who reads in an inaudible voice for seven or eight minutes and announces last week's 'offering for God's work was eight shillings and sixpence'.

sex

What people in Kensington have their coal delivered in.

surplice

Nightie. Nightshirt. Negligee, etc. Best on top of day wear.

111

surplus

Not known in church.

shrine

What the little old lady who polishes the church brass is hoping for. Or chorus: 'Shrine Jesus, shrine, etc.

statue

1. The normal question asked by the congregation of their neighbour during the carols by candlelight service.
2. Liturgical sneeze.

statute

A pillar. A law. A revealed truth from on high. A basic canonical tenet without which the entire insitution of the church will fall apart, its fabric rent asunder. For example: Never Interrupt The Minister During His Sermon Even If He Is Talking Patent and Utter Tosh.

Smithwulf

Bishop of London, 860 AD.

slowing

Opposite of fasting. And rather more common.

Songs of Fellowship

Best heard at a football ground between 3 and 5 pm on Saturdays.

spirituality

The art of making connections.

share

Gossip.

sacred dance

(*See* DRAMA GROUP.)

shriven

The state of having confessed your sin and been absolved by a priest.

shrivelled

The opposite of the above.

sermon

A forgotten art that many preachers try to remember on a Sunday morning—and fail.

sermon in song
Vicar/minister leaves his mike on during hymns.

sermonette
Talk lasting less than twenty minutes.

sermon chanted evening
Vicar does talk in funny and flat sing-song voice.

Sunday school address
Same as church (don't forget the postcode).

screen, rood
Used to cover up the church's rood bits.

stall, choir
When fat lady singer gets jammed between the pews and the other singers can't get by.

service book
A service manual like you get with your car that you ignore until you are completely baffled, broken down or confused.

silence
To rendezvous with the still, small voice.

saint
Sinner in disguise.

sinner
Saint in waiting.

sect
No sects please, we're British.

sectarian

One who cannot get sects off his mind. A veritable sects maniac.

soul friend

Someone who offers you a safe place to unpack your bags, emotional and spiritual—in order to see what you're carrying around. They then help you decide what's useful and what's not, what's good and what's not, what's true and what's not. (Pronounced: 'Freedom'.)

sale, jumble

Opportunity for church members to: 1. feel they're environmentally right-on in re-cycling Mrs Jones' broken sandals, even though she had verrucas; 2. feel they're socially benefiting the less well-off; 3. help pay for a few slates on the new roof.

so-be-it

Religious version of 'All-right-if-that's-the-way-you-want-to-play-it-matey...'.

stations of the cross

King's Cross, Charing Cross, etc.

stations, British Rail

Ideal venues for open-air evangelism on Saturday morning.

Salvation Army

People in hats and uniforms who make tea and play trumpets at Christmas.

server

Christ or Christ-ians.

streetwise

Some ten years ago, this attitude replaced holiness as 'that which is most necessary for salvation'. To be 'more streetwise than thou' is the ambition of all believers.

sound

In agreement with me.

saved

Uses the same Christian bookshop as me.

Spirit-filled

Uses the same song book as me.

Shalamar Yamaha Kawasaki Honda

speaking in tongues

(*See* previous entry.)

Satan

Also known as The Crowbar, because he separates people from people and people from God.

stipend

From the Latin 'Stipius Pendere', meaning 'You cannot be serious!' 'Stipend' denotes something very small, something pitifully derisory, tiny, inadequate. Something miserably insufficient, pathetically weedy. First used to describe clergy pay in 1753 and the name has stuck.

sin

As in, 'Whatsinitforme?'

sinspiration

Another tortuous sermon illustration.

spire

The whole point of a church. (*See* INSPIRE.)

slype

A passage from a cathedral transept to a chapter house or deanery. That piece of information is going to enrich your life, isn't it?

Songs of Praise

A scheme provided by the BBC to fill every church in Britain with happy smiling people...at least once every 100 years.

Sunday school

A small therapy group comprised of victims of parental churchgoing.

stained-glass windows

What you get after the Sunday school do painting lessons.

small change

(*See* OFFERING.)

small change, very

(*See* above.)

synod

War zone.

sack

That which contains potatoes.

sacraments

That which contains God's love. Church history suggests

that there are somewhere between 0 and 43 recognised
sacraments of the church, indicating that they are either
soul-bendingly important or completely peripheral. Or
both. Or neither. Let the burning continue.

share

To whinge in public.

shalabalom

Paul Daniels' magic word.

shalom

God's magic word.

society

Place just outside the church which many churchgoers, with
meetings every day of the week, never actually get to see.

self

The bit many churchgoers like to condemn all the time—

evil, self-ish, generally not too good, etc. Also the bit Jesus said to love as much as our neighbour.

salvation

The final hymn.

success

An increasing ease with failure.

Sunday school attendant

(*See* BATS.)

swarthy

Dusky, dark skinned, of a dark Hugh (Ed: 'Sorry?'). As used in that famous and popular indiginous African song: 'Swarthy, Swarthy, Swarthy is the Lord...'

systematic theology

'The devil's way to spread Christianity' (Munk).

slim for him

Slogan of the popular Spiritual Aerobics Movement based on John the Baptist's words, 'He must become greater and greater, I must become less and less.'

slim hymn

Chorus.

thousand, one hundred and forty-four

A little bigger than the MORRIS THOUSAND.

tablet

What God gave Moses to cure his headaches with the Israelites. Take two three times a day after meals.

temptation

The deluded 'If only...' of the hungry soul.

televangelism

A sacred way to go to prison.

travelling expenses

A small sum of money paid by a church to a visiting speaker that bears no relation to the actual cost of keeping a car on the road.

testament

It ain't half a Bible. (Well, it is really.)

theology

The ology which pertains to seeing above. See below.

theological college

Logical college to go to if you see above (or want to). See above.

theological seminary

(*See* SEE ABOVE.) Above.

theological cemetery

Where they turn 'God Is Dad' theology into 'God Is Dead' theology.

Thought for the Day

An annoying, over-cheerful person who comes on Radio 4
in the morning in order to give Brian Redhead time to go to
the loo, who makes you realise it is high time to turn off the
radio and get into the shower. As in: 'I was walking down
the street the other day and a man came up to me and
said...' (Turn radio off. Shower on.)

trophy of grace

Mature and much-admired Christian.

thurible

A vessel in which incense is burnt—so-called because it
smells absolutely thurible.

team ministry

B: OK, Jack, you can have the church building at 10.00 am
on Sunday.

M: No he can't, Barry.

B: I'm sorry, Margaret?

M: Jack *can't* have it at 10.00 am on Sundays because *I've*
got it at 10.00 am on Sundays.

J: No, Margaret, you've got the *daughter* church complex
at 10.00 am.

M: No, I've got the daughter church complex at 8.00 am.

B: You *what*?

M: We agreed.

B: I'm afraid we most certainly did *not* agree. *I've* got the
daughter church complex at 8.00 am. *You've* got it at
10.00 am.

M: Well, really!

J: And another thing—who's got use of the verger this
week?

M: Me.

B: Margaret, you had full use of the verger all *last* month.

M: It was a short month—he was sick one week.

J: Really, Barry, I do feel that Margaret should hand over
the verger *immediately*... (etc, etc.)

te deum laudamus

Tedium louder must we?

testimony

An extraordinary, far-fetched story of long, long ago, with
the most exciting part at the beginning and the dull bit at
the end—unlike most stories—whereby the teller
spellbinds a congregation with a fantastic tale of debauched
sex, drugs and rock 'n roll, drink, gambling, dancing,
wickedness, sin and insider dealing at great length and in
the greatest detail—leaving nothing whatsoever to the
imagination. At the end of which he or she says that they
don't, of course, do any of those things any more—and the
whole congregation thinks to themselves, 'What a shame—
sounded exciting.'

the word of the Lord

To most people the word of the Lord is 'No'. In fact it may
more often be found to be 'Yes'. And occasionally, 'Leave
it with me, I'll get back to you on that one.'

two or three

Expression taken from a Bible verse which is much quoted
when numbers are disappointingly low.

tower

A very large architectural feature pioneered by the
Babylonians to enable themselves to get on more even
terms with God. Nowadays left for the birds.

tower of power

Invention of American TV evangelists—believed to be
where they store the cash sent in to them by widows and
orphans.

thou

King James' term of endearment for the Almighty. As in, 'It's for thou...'

thee

Sixteenth-century term still wowing them in Welsh non-conformist chapels. As in, 'We, thine unworthy servants beseech thee...heretofore, and hereunto, and hereafter most unworthily that thou wouldst holpen thine humble servantage to communicatest thine great gospel to yonder ordinary man in the street.'

thy

(*See* THIGH.)

this is the day

This is the day that we sing that same old song again. What day was it again?

total immersion

The pipes in the church kitchen have burst again.

traditionalist

Awkward old boy/girl. Found in most churches. Give-away sign: minimalist vocabulary—usually just the one word, 'No'.

thus saith the Lord...

Don't you dare disagree with this!

tithe

Conclusive proof that the average churchgoer earns around £10.00 a week.

time of testing

Minister meeting with the Scout Master concerning the National Anthem in the Parade Service.

temptation

The thought of where the Scout Master ought to go.

tract

Short but sensitively worded pamphlet that gently expounds a person's need for God.

transept

Apply a plaster and some Savlon if it gets nasty.

trance

Makes you go cross-eyed.

tambourine

Makes you go deaf.

team leader

Makes you wish you'd gone deaf.

treasurer

Short arms, deep pockets.

thigh

'Thigh be the Glory...' Sung in praise of Rosemary Conley, author of the best selling *Hip And Thy Diet*.

television evangelist

Man in prison.

under the blood

The kind of easy-to-understand phrase tract-writers like to use. Something to do with vampires and churchyards at night?

under the table

Where you find teetotal preachers after they have taken a Communion service at an unfamiliar church.

undecided

State of being under the blankets in a warm bed at 10.30 am on a Sunday morning. (*See also* UNDER THE DUVET.)

undertaker

The man on the take when you go under.

unhelpful

Young people's comments after yet another dull church service.

USA

A country famous for its churchgoing and for the absence of God.

up yonder, way

The Next Life. The Afterlife. Next Bit. Part Two. The Main Event. A Large House With Many Rooms Where We're All Going To Eat Apple Pie In The Sky.

unity

Other people joining in with what we're doing.

unc

Religious word for oil.

unction

One of the lesser known words from 'Give me oil in my lamp': the verse, 'Give me unction for my gumption / Let me function, function, function...'

ungrateful

The majority of all churchgoers judging by the average amount put into the collection plate each week.

ungodly

Being in a state of not being very much like God. Most of us, much of the time.

ungod

Old Nick, the Devil, Satan, Luci.

ungent

(That's enough Ungs. Ed.)

unctuous

Oily. Sounds unpleasant. See above.

usher

The person, usually a man, whose job it is to make sure you

are not talking loudly by the time you get to your seat in church—because apparently God doesn't like you talking at a normal volume. His job is to get a bit of 'ush—hence usher. If you're still talking he'll be the one—along with many others—who glare at you. Sometimes the usher becomes the rusher. This may happen when someone drunk or otherwisely embarrassing slips into church and needs to be shown the door in a smart fashion—sometimes shouting rude words about Christians being supposed to help the needy—in which case the rusher becomes the usher again.

Überlieferungsgeshichte

A German theological word, denoting hard moral advice given. As in, 'Überlieferungsgeschichte? That's easy for *you* to say!'

vestibule

A baggy undergarment. (*See* VESTRY.)

virtue

Shown not in abstaining from sin—but in not desiring it.

vertical thinking

Prayer.

verger

A verger looks after the church cleaning, maintenance and day-to-day running. It's a bit of a duff job and not very well paid so the best person for the job is someone on the verger the grave.

verger's wand

A rod, often with decorated head, carried by vergers as a symbol of their authority.

verger's baseball bat

A baseball bat, generally without a decorated head, carried by vergers to enforce their authority.

vicarage

Place for storing vicars, usually one at a time. Found next to many Anglican church buildings. Tell-tale sign: general state of structural dilapidation and large sacks of rubbish left on front door by parishioners who believe they are doing the church a favour and call it 'jumble'.

vineyard, this corner of the Lord's

A pious phrase used lovingly by church secretaries in giving the notices. Literal meaning: 'Here'.

vestry

Small room often at front of church building. Not unlike Superman's phone-box but in this case a man in a scruffy suit with a briefcase goes in and, seconds later, a man in a dress and a dog-collar comes out and starts leading the service.

video, wedding

The seemingly obligatory creative, emotional and spiritual disaster, perpetrated by the depressingly drunk Uncle Dick. In theory, a record for posterity of the moment two become one in the marriage service. In reality, Uncle Dick rarely gets up in time for this but *does* get to the wedding reception. Once there, and having made himself a secure base at the bar, he makes occasional sorties out into the crowd concentrating increasingly on some of the prettier teenage nieces present. Along with Uncle Dick's thumb, the bride and groom may also appear.

voluntary

Word often used by other members of your church in describing a service they are inviting you to perform on a weekly basis for ever ... for the Lord. Often used simultaneously with the ecclesiastical exercise known as 'Twisting of the Arm'.

verily, verily, verily

All right, listen up...

vicar

A qualified juggler.

vestments

Frocks for men.

volunteer

Somebody else.

Vatican

Small city in Rome full of big buildings filled with fabulous treasures where men wander round wearing valuable religious jewellery. People who live in the Vatican are followers of the Son of Man who had nowhere to lay his head. One of those ironic twists of history.

vatman

Vatican Man, the Pope.

venerable

Word used to describe an elderly clergyman who has obviously gone stark raving bonkers and completely senile. As in: 'I'm afraid the Revd Clitheroe is no more than a venerable these days.'

vestry

Something warm you wear under your shirtry.

vicar

Assistant to below.

vicar's wife

Officially the person in charge of an Anglican church. Charged with the task of looking after the souls of the parishioners, running women's meetings and arranging the arrangements for the flower arranging.

vicar's family

A term for anyone who is patient, long-suffering or put-upon.

virgin

A biblical concept once popular, virtually unknown today.

visitation

You know you are about to die when you get a visitation from your minister. Alternatively you will know that you are already dead.

wedding

Short religious event where a man and a woman ask God to bless their joined-up hearts, followed by photographic ceremony in church grounds lasting several days.

worthy

A word often used by Christian hymn writers who are stuck for a rhyme in the last verse. Works reasonably well with:
HOLY
O THEE
YOU AND ME
SWARTHY
ROLY POLY, etc.

walking with the Lord

Egalitarian spiritual experience, notable in that this kind of walking does not exclude the halt, the lame, the limp or the wheelchair-bound.

weather cock

Turns and changes according to the wind direction. But not necessarily Anglican.

weather vane

A weathercock with a mirror and comb.

wake

> Procedure which takes place in some countries after a
> death. A lot of people cry very loudly, hence the
> expression, 'Loud enough to wake the dead.'

wedding photographs

> An expensive and exhausting photographic session aimed at
> making the newly married couple and guests look as unlike
> themselves as possible—with the specific intention of
> embarrassing everyone pictured therein for years to come
> and eliciting the comment 'Who was that?!', the correct
> answer being 'me'.

wise man

> Built his house upon the rock...and managed to sell it
> before the housing slump.

wise men

> The chaps who position themselves in the gallery at the
> evening service the better to see the women below.

wise virgins

> The women who do the above, to see the above, to do
> nothing with the above.

warden, church

> Annoying ecclesiastic (Anglican) liable to book you for
> illegal pew-parking.

warden, traffic

> Last year's winner of the Most Prayed Against Person
> Award.

wee frees

> Affectionate nickname for small Scottish denomination, the
> Free Presbyterians. (*See also* WE FREE KINGS.)

Whitsun

Refers to the sending down of the Holy Spirit upon the disciples at Pentecost. Also used by keen clerics who, in seeking the gifts of the Spirit, may be heard to remark, 'I just don't know what to do. Frankly I'm at my whitsun.'

word in season

In church, a word in season for winter is 'Brrrrrrr'.

word from the Lord, a

Otherwise known as, 'Now I don't want to be contradicted on this one...'

whither goest thou?

Minister who uses Authorized Version of the Bible speaking to his son as he sees him driving off in the car.

whitherheckdoyouthinkyou'vebeen?

Same minister as his son arrives back courtesy of a pick-up truck at 2 am.

wallet

Unique area in popular Christian theology: alone in entire universe and galaxies beyond it where God is believed not to be.

women

Don't see under P for priests.

women of prayer

Female version of Men of God.

will

Extraordinary popular character in hymnbooks, where churchgoers are regularly asked to pledge to his will, etc.

wayside pulpit

Rickety wooden notice-board bearing a subtle message in angry day-glo colours to 'The World'—for instance 'Turn or burn' or 'Eternity is a long time in hell, O wretched sinners!' etc, etc. (It is unclear how effective the wayside pulpit is as an evangelistic tool.)

world

Good enough to be worth saving. Bad enough to need Christ to do it.

weather

Common topic of conversation after church by people too nervous or retiring to talk about something substantial, like what to do about the minister's sermon on Simple Lifestyles. Eg 'It's the greenhouse effect, you know... it's all in Revelation, of course.'

whisper

Common ecclesiastical practice and enjoying something of a revival in charismatically-inclined congregations where you may often turn to the person next to you, thinking they are trying to attract your attention during prayers, only to discover they are 'in the Spirit'.

xstatic utterances

(*See* S for SHALAMAR YAMAHA KAWASAKI HONDA.)

xylophone

1960s trendy church instrument.

Xmas

Crossmass. A special time for arguments, the renewal of family feuds, the uncovering of old sores. A time for sitting alone at home wishing you weren't alone and feeling angry and cross.

x-tacy

(Spelled ecstacy) Alternative to getting drunk on the alcoholic spirit—getting drunk on the Holy Spirit.

ex-nihilo

Literally means: 'Out of nothing'. Usual context for this term is 'God created the universe ex-nihilo.' However other uses include, 'The two ministers were making an argument ex-nihilo.'

young wives

Any wife who is no longer young.

yolk

Usually cracked during a sermon and never funny. But this doesn't stop those who are awake from laughing—probably humouring the preacher to prevent more of the same.

Youth Praise

A brave attempt to bring church music up to date. It managed to bring it right up as far as the 1960s and left it marooned there, gasping.

youth of today, the

The traditional shorthand applied to every consecutive generation without exception since two thousand years before Christ—a witless, insensitive, loutish, loud, arrogant, brash bunch of no-hopers the like of which you have never seen...er, since you were that age.

youth work

Talking to a young person in a down-to-earth, unpatronising sort of way.

youth rally

Talking to lots of people in a down-to-earth unpatronising sort of way.

youth service

Patronising them again.

youth nite

A Saturday evening 'meeting' planned, entitled, prayed for, organised, led and attended entirely by middle-aged churchgoers. Other titles include: Tots, Teens 'n Twenties; A Special Young Person's Evening and the classic Youth for Christ Rally.

York

Number Two in the See Chart. Just ahead of London and just behind this week's number one, Canterbury.

yule

Famous Christian football hymn: 'Yule never walk alone.'

you, and also with

An ecclesiastical way of saying 'And the same to you.' A useful riposte when finding yourself in a strange church and not understanding anything that is being said to you.

zion, language of

(*See* this entire book.)

zeal

What young people ought to have.

zest

What they ought to wash with.

Zoroastrian

Non-Christian religion...but starts with a Z.

zinc

Er, we're a bit short on Z's.

Zacchaeus

A man in the Bible most famous for being short. He also drank tea and was given to climbing trees, apparently.

ZZZZZZZZZ's

In abundance during sermons, often silent. Tell-tale signs: closed eyes but grunts and snores indicate this is not for prayer.

Zion

Name of several thousand non-conformist chapels in South Wales.

Zebedee

Disciple of Jesus with the gift of the best name.

The

English-Church

Dictionary

All members of the clergy speak in tongues—as we've seen from the preceding pages. However, it isn't unknown for someone who sits in the church pew to be misunderstood by the clergy. It works both ways. Quite often people who never go to church have difficulty in getting through to their local minister. Here are some words and phrases that you might use with interpretations for the clergy.

alleluia!

'I hope this sounds suitably spiritual.'

Amen

'Right, this has gone on long enough.'

I'm bored

This means that in spite of hours spent in careful sermon preparation, the careful development of the argument, the precise use of words and the beautiful elocution, enunciation and projection, the sermon has failed to hold me. In fact it never grabbed me in the first place.

Lovely sermon, Vicar

'I don't know what to say to you because you are dressed up in strange clothes, in a strange building, talking in strange terms about strange things. I don't know where to begin and I don't think I'll bother to find out, either. So I'll just get out of here as quickly and painlessly as possible. What's for lunch, I wonder?'

Thank you for asking, Pastor. I'm fine

'I'm fouled up, insecure, neurotic, emotional. . . .'

See you next week, perhaps

'You won't see me next week. Or ever, perhaps.'

Good holiday, Pastor?

'I wonder why you bothered to return, Pastor.'

Thank you for your address

'I knew you lived at the Manse anyway.'

Now that's what I call a sermon, Reverend

'I wonder if once, just once, we could have one that comes in under two hours.'

Another cucumber sandwich, Vicar?

'Don't they have food at the Vicarage?'

More tea, Vicar?

'Surely five cups were enough? *When* are you going to go?'

You were in fine voice this morning, Pastor

'Can't you remember to turn your flippin' microphone off during the hymns?'

Your sermon was like God's mercy and God's peace

'It was endless and passed all understanding.'

I'm sure one of those newcomers in the congregation plays the piano. Wouldn't your wife appreciate the odd week off?

'The congregation would certainly love the odd week off!'

Little Johnny didn't seem to want to go to Sunday school this morning. I don't know why

'Yes I do. He doesn't go a bundle on the flannelgraph.'

You know we give by direct debit now. Don't you, Minister?

'Is there any way you can stop that plonker with the collection plate from glaring at us every week as if we don't pay our way—we do give sacrifically you know?'

I know you're a very busy man, Reverend

'*Please* don't come to visit me.'

I love that suit you're wearing, Vicar

'*We* gave that suit to the jumble sale, you know.'

That new chorus seems to be a big hit

   'Did we have to sing that chorus twenty-five times non-stop?'

I've never quite understood the doctrine of substitutionary atonement before

   'And I still don't.'

Was the heating on today, Vicar?

   'Why the heck wasn't the heating on today?'

I'm sorry we can't stay for the church lunch

   'Thank goodness we've got visitors today.'

You have a very fine church building

   'Is it really so impossible to make the service more interesting?'

This speaking in tongues during the service seems to be catching on

   'I'm off.'

That talk really spoke to me, Reverend

   'Yes, it said, "Get out of here while the going's good." '

That talk really spoke to me, Reverend

   'Yes, and it spoke to me last month, too.'

I do believe God has marked this place for revival

   'This place really is the pits, isn't it?'

What an intriguing illustration about the cows of Bashan, Pastor

   'Was it strictly necessary to bring the livestock into the church this morning—and who's on the cleaning rota?'

Now that's what I call a flower arrangement

'For some reason I'm reminded of *The Day of the Triffids*.

I thought your sermon was *marvellous*

'Your sermon made me feel superior to nearly all my friends.'

That was a brave and courageous sermon, Vicar

'You're nuts.'

Curate, you must be tired of living off baked beans on your own. Would you like to come round soon for some nice home cooking?

'I've always seen myself as a vicar's wife. This boy looks promising.'

Curate, what exactly are your views on divine guidance?

'God has told me to marry you.'

Of course, I speak only as a layman

'That sermon was a load of tosh.'

The new PA system is very sophisticated, isn't it?

'We never had all those hums and squeaks before.'

How's the Appeal Fund going, Vicar?

'Rain water was dripping on my head again this morning.'

It's always so refreshing when the Youth Group takes the service

'If I'd known I would have stayed at home.'

Could you remind me of the dates for the local March for Jesus, Vicar?

'We need to book some holiday that weekend.'

Ah yes, Johnny told me that, er, a 'Man of the Cloth' had visited his school today

'Had another extra-terrestrial in assembly today, dad.'

You really laid it on the line this morning, Pastor

'Phew! *Thank goodness* we didn't bring the neighbours!'

You look as if you need a break, Reverend

'I need a break, Reverend.'

Interesting way to illustrate the leap of faith, Pastor

'You'll be in plaster for weeks.'

Interesting choice of hymns, Vicar

'Do you choose them in your sleep?'

You have many friends in the community

'I don't actually like you very much.'

You've certainly made an impact in the locality, Pastor

'I don't think *anyone* likes you very much.'

Speaking on the book of Amos again this morning?

'Have you joined the Communist Party yet?'

I see the curate is preaching from the Song of Solomon next week, Vicar

'Is he really old enough to be reading that kind of thing?'

How did you feel about the use of sacred dance this evening, Vicar?

'All those girls in leotards seem to have raised the temperature of the congregation somewhat. We're going to have to watch this trend.'

You're a very compassionate man

'Have you always found decision-making difficult?'

Is that you, Father?

'With all this incense, I can't see a thing!'

The new music group seems to be entering into the spirit of things here at St Swithins

'You don't think that three heavy metal guitarists and two drummers is a little over the top, do you...?'

What would the bishop say if he walked in?

'We'll soon find out. I'm off to tell him.'

I don't think I've ever heard that tune we sang to the third hymn

'...And neither had anyone else.'

101 Things To Do During A Dull Sermon

by Tim Sims & Dan Pegoda

Sermons are great…most of the time. But when your minister has a bad day, and the minutes grind by, surviving to the last 'and finally' can be a tough business. Here are 101 wonderful exercises to keep boredom at bay.

For example:

- Pass a note to the organist asking whether he or she plays requests.
- See if a yawn is really contagious.
- Slap your neighbour. See if he or she turns the other cheek. If not, raise your hand and tell the pastor.
- Try to guess what the sidesmen are doing in the vestry.
- Devise ways of climbing into the balcony without using the stairs.

Author **TIM SIMS** has been chaplain of Death Valley National Park, and now holds a dull job in a dull university. Illustrator **DAN PEGODA** began drawing on church pews at the age of three. He is now art director of *The Wittenburg Door*.

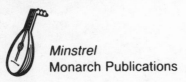

Minstrel
Monarch Publications

101 Things To Do With A Dull Church

by Martin Wroe & Adrian Reith

Church is exciting...stimulating...thrilling. In theory.

The Award Winning Team that brought you *101 Things To Do During A Dull Sermon* now bring you a searing, soaring, sanctimonious selection of sizzling solutions to sort out your church's every dull moment.

No theological training establishment should be without it.

Includes:
* Prayer on the loss or mislaying of a filofax
* Short service of blessing for those approaching baldness
* How to cure your minister's terrible 'preaching voice'
* How to raise millions through a single jumble sale
* How to deal with a stroppy church meeting
* How to lead a Bible study—without being there

Martin Wroe is a tall man. Adrian Reith is not. They have both slept through thousands of church services...and stayed awake in several others. Together they founded the Burning Books empire. Martin is a freelance journalist. Adrian is a writer and producer of commercials. Together they have The Ministry of Mirth.

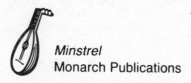

Minstrel
Monarch Publications

The '101' Survivor's Guide to The Church

by Martin Wroe, Nick McIvor and Simon Parke

'Funnier than your minister's preaching voice and with more flare than his trousers.'

Includes:
The ASB – Alternative Sermon Book
Situations Vacant – Could you be the next Billy Graham?
Christian Bestsellers – a bluffer's guide to after-church conversation
The Not Too Good Church Guide – St John The Power Evangelist, or
The Church of God's Bounty in the Home Counties?

'In an age when nine out of ten people prefer to lie in bed or to wash the car on a Sunday morning, a vicar and a church warden have compiled a guide on how to survive a church service. The Guide, aimed at ordained ministers, lay members and non-church goers, gives advice on what to do in almost any eventuality, including being asked unexpectedly to preach a sermon. The book also explains how to interest an absent congregation and how to get "one of those funny preaching voices" . . .

'The book is designed to elucidate the theological gobbledegook and explain how to distinguish between the 60,000 churches in the UK. Martin Wroe, a church warden . . . denies that the guide is irreverent. "We are not poking fun at the essential Christian beliefs; we are poking fun at the inessential Christian beliefs, especially those associated with churchgoing.

'"In theory, the idea of churchgoing is marvellous. Unfortunately, in most churches it is a dull, anaesthetised experience where you come out feeling worse than when you went in . . ."'
(From an article in The Times, August 1990)

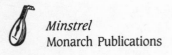

Minstrel
Monarch Publications